# SENTINELS OF TIME

## Vermont's Covered Bridges

### By Phil Ziegler

Down East Books • Camden, Maine 04843

ISBN 0-89272-160-X
Library of Congress Catalog Card Number 82-73601
Design by Karen Searls
Composition by Roxmont Graphics
Printed in the United States of America

10   9   8   7   6   5   4   3   2

Down East Books
Camden, Maine 04843

To my wife, Betty Lou,
whose patience, criticism, and inspiration
made this book a work of love.

# Contents

Acknowledgments    ix

Introduction    2

Types of Trusses and Their Inventors    4

The Portals    6

Addison County    9

Bennington County    13

Caledonia County    17

Chittenden County    25

Essex County    29

Franklin County    33

Lamoille County    43

Orange County    63

Orleans County    73

Rutland County    81

Washington County    89

Windham County    105

Windsor County    121

# Acknowledgments

In the past many months, I have counted on the help of a number of people who have shared with me their expertise and precious memorabilia. I wish to thank Mr. Neal Templeton of Brattleboro, Vermont, for his unlimited help and encouragement; Mr. Wendell Smith of the Vermont State Highway Department who loaned me his collection of old post cards; Mr. Joseph Conwill of Reading, Pennsylvania, for placing his trust in a complete stranger by sending me his marvelous collection of photographs and for sharing his encyclopedic knowledge of covered bridges with me; Raymond and Barbara Brainerd of Brandon, Vermont, for sharing photographs and information with me; and Cedric Reynolds of South Burlington, Vermont, for his many old pictures and for guiding me through the many technical aspects of covered bridges. Special thanks to Mr. Richard Roy of Manchester, New Hampshire, for loaning me over three hundred personal photographs and for the expert information he gave me concerning these bridges and to Mr. Richard Sanders Allen for the use of his book, *Covered Bridges of the Northeast*, which gave me much useful information.

Thank you to the Connecticut River Valley Covered Bridge Society for the use of their bulletins in gleaning much information that I could not find elsewhere.

Lastly, thanks to Mr. Herbert Wheaton Congdon for writing his beautiful book, *The Covered Bridge, an Old Landmark*, which gave me invaluable background and kept my spirits afloat throughout this project.

Phil Ziegler
1982

What stories could these bridges tell
If they could only talk?
They'd tell us of the ones who rode
And those who had to walk,
The rich, the poor . . . those in-between
Who used their planks to cross,
The soldiers, farmers, businessmen
In buggies, sleighs, by "hoss,"
Like sentinels these bridges stand
In spite of flood and fire,
Their rugged, stalwart strength remains
Our future to inspire.

# Introduction

The sole purpose of this book is to bring to you some of the moments of happiness and tranquility these grand old covered bridges have brought to me.

This is not a book dealing with the principles involved in the construction of covered bridges, nor is it intended to be a historical tome. Many, many books have already been written on these subjects, so I will not repeat that technical data here. Nor is this work a catalogue of every covered bridge still standing in Vermont. Nearly a third of the bridges pictured here have already succumbed to time and neglect. Others still in existence either have been so greatly altered or else are so nearly identical to bridges already included that I decided to omit them.

This is a memorial to those special old covered bridges which have, long since, passed into history and a monument to those still serving the people of Vermont.

Many years ago, an incident occurred which, in a way, planted the seed which grew into this book. It was a beautiful summer day. The surrounding mountains beckoned me to look upward, as if, in so doing, I would always be rewarded with happiness and tranquility. At the time, I was standing at the portal of a lovely

moss-covered bridge. A stranger was about to cross over it, and I remarked on the beauty of the bridge. He looked at me like I was visitor from outer space and said, "Why, this ain't nothin' but a big old barn with a hole at each end and nothin' in the middle. All it's good fer is to git me from one side of the river to the other." And, with that, he walked across the bridge shaking his head and muttering to himself. Here he was in the presence of history and yet blind to the fact that for over a hundred years this "big old barn" had been a portal to commerce.

I immediately began to wonder how many people who depended upon these old landmarks could so take them for granted. It became clear to me that I wanted, in some way, to bring the beauty and the tremendous value to our well being to the fore and, perhaps, contribute my share by revealing to the average person what an essential part these covered bridges play in preserving the historical heritage of Vermont.

As you view the drawings in this book, you will notice that, unlike a portfolio of photographs which would tend to make one bridge look exactly like the next, each bridge here takes on a personality of its own. The surrounding foliage, the rocks and boulders, the quiet flow of the streams and rivers these covered bridges span, and the backdrops of mountains paint a scene of unique beauty.

Like some people, these old bridges age with grace. Many have had a face-lift or, perhaps, two or three, as wrinkles in the form of rotted boards and underpinning began to appear. Holes formed in the roofs. Many began to lean to either side as their legs became weak with age. With quite a number, renovation has thwarted the signs of old age. Still, like numerous older citizens, too many have been left alone — to be passed by and forgotten.

As in the floods of 1927, which wiped out nearly half of the bridges in Vermont, nature can be devastating. Fortunately, some of these bridges were so sturdily built, they were set up again where they landed down river. At other original sites, the main "stringers" (those heavy beams upon which the bridges were originally placed) were left intact, and parts of other bridges were salvaged to reconstruct covered bridges on these sites. Many are still standing.

By 1946, there were 170 covered bridges still in use in Vermont. Today, there are less than 114, and the figure is dwindling every day. Although Vermont has more covered bridges in use than all the other New England states combined, it stands fourth among the states in the number left.

A dedicated few are working diligently towards preserving those covered bridges which remain. Perhaps this book will reach those people who "just don't care," before they allow even one more covered bridge to be destroyed and replaced with a steel-and-concrete bridge — which won't last nearly as long and may cost ten times as much!

I urge the people who read this book who have never visited one of these splendid old covered bridges to do so on a quiet afternoon when an uplift is in order. The music of the stream as it flows under the cool shade of the bridge may seem to be a symphony of peace, and the world with all of its troubles and catastrophes can, for the moment, be forgotten.

Look closely at each drawing in this book. Experience the quiet dignity and the sensation of passing history. Savor the softness of the moss-covered boards, the cool foliage, and the surrounding trees and mountains. In less than a half-hour's drive, in almost any direction, you may find one. Do it while you can. They are disappearing quickly, and when they are all gone, nothing in the world will ever take their place.

# Types of Trusses and Their Inventors

As you go through this book, you will find a description of each bridge and, in most cases, the type of construction used to build it. To make it easier for you to picture the different types of trusses used in these bridges, you will find a sketch of each type in the following drawings.

Most of the basic designs were originally put on paper by a young Italian engineer, Andre Palladio, who was born in Vicenza in Northern Italy in 1580. He is credited by many historians as being the grandfather of the covered bridge.

Timothy Palmer patented his Arched truss in 1797, followed by Theodore Burr, who patented the Burr truss in 1804. Ethiel Town patented the truss bearing his name, the Town Lattice truss, in 1820. It was the first truly new design and had tremendous strength.

The most productive of all the designers and patentees of covered bridges was Stephen H. Long, born in Hopkinton, New Hampshire, in 1784. He was more interested in promoting the covered bridge than building it, and for about ten years, his was the most sought after design by bridge builders concerned with supporting tremendous loads such as railroad traffic.

Soon after, William Howe, born in 1803, came upon the scene, and his patented Howe truss became the favorite design for covered-bridge builders from Maine to California.

**Ten of the Most Common Types of Trusses Used in the Construction of Covered Bridges**

5

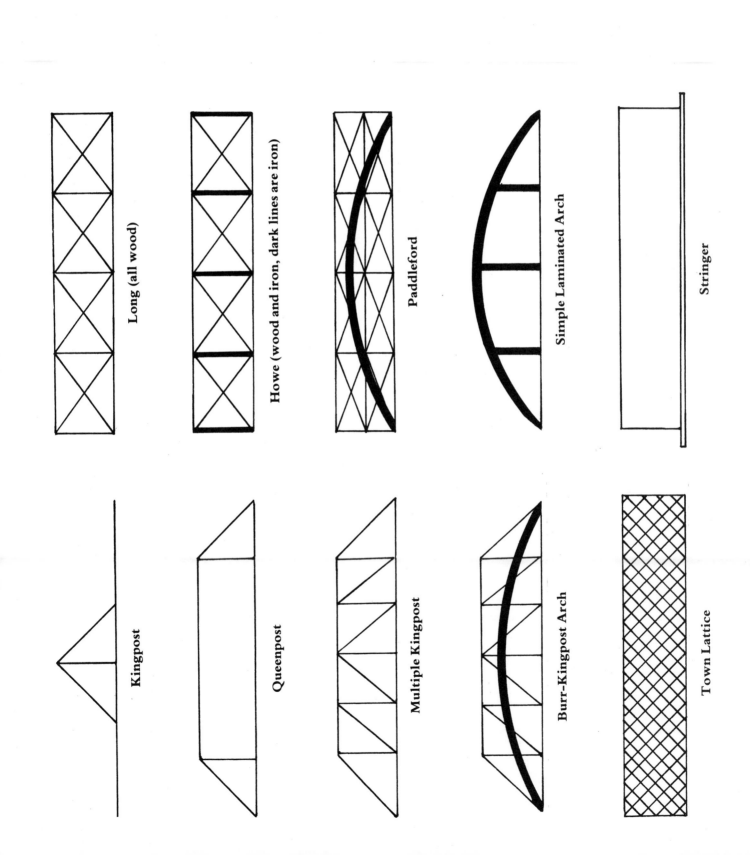

Kingpost

Queenpost

Multiple Kingpost

Burr-Kingpost Arch

Town Lattice

Long (all wood)

Howe (wood and iron, dark lines are iron)

Paddleford

Simple Laminated Arch

Stringer

# The Portals

Each builder of covered bridges hoped to make his bridge unique. The treatment of the portals, the entrances to the bridges, made this possible. If not for the portals, each covered bridge truly could look like the next. The following sketches are from Richard Sanders Allen's wonderful book, *Covered Bridges of the Northeast*, and with his permission, I have drawn elevations of them here.

## Representative Portals

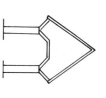
Bennett Bridge
Wilson's Mill, Maine

Lovejoy Bridge
South Andover, Maine

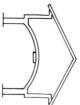
Albany, New Hampshire

County Farm Bridge
Dover, New Hampshire

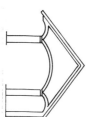
Lyndonville, Vermont

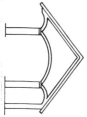
Creamery Bridge
Brattleboro, Vermont

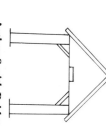
Arthur Smith Bridge
Lyonsville, Massachusetts

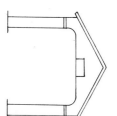
West Cornwall, Connecticut

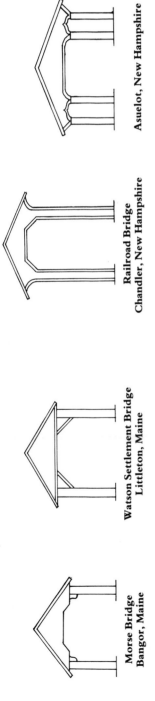

**Morse Bridge**
**Bangor, Maine**

**Watson Settlement Bridge**
**Littleton, Maine**

**Railroad Bridge**
**Chandler, New Hampshire**

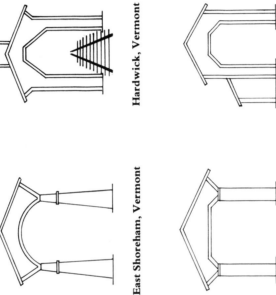

**Asuelot, New Hampshire**

**Mechanic St. Bridge**
**Lancaster, New Hampshire**

**Northfield Falls, Vermont**

**East Shoreham, Vermont**

**Hardwick, Vermont**

**Museum Bridge**
**Shelburne, Vermont**

**Pumping Station Bridge**
**Greenfield, Massachusetts**

**Gilbertville, Massachusetts**

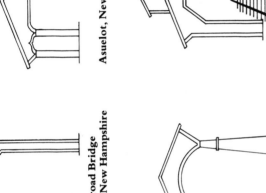

**East Pepperell, Massachusetts**

**Blenheim Bridge**
**North Blenheim, New York**

**Cemetery Bridge**
**Troy, New York**

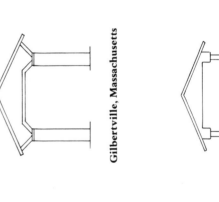
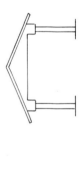
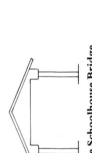
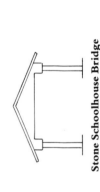
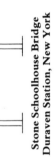

**Stone Schoolhouse Bridge**
**Duraven Station, New York**

**Grant's Mills Bridge**
**Arena, New York**

# ADDISON COUNTY

In Shoreham Center you will find the Rutland Railroad Bridge. Built in 1887 of Howe truss costruction, it spans 108 feet across Lemon Fair River. The rail line has long since been abandoned, but the bridge still remains west off Route 7, at Whiting, just off the Shoreham Center Road.

Phil
Ziegler
82

(*Left*)  Lewis Creek Bridge stood in North Ferrisburg. Little is remembered about this bridge. It was moved near the Old Farm Restaurant on Route 7 in Ferrisburg as a tourist attraction.

(*Right*)  The Pulp Mill Bridge, a two-way bridge, was built in 1812 by an unknown builder, and completely restored as of 1980. Of Burr Arch construction, it has a span of 179 feet over Otter Creek, near Middlebury, on the Middlebury-Weybridge Road. It is one of only two of its kind left in Vermont. The other, the former Cambridge Bridge, is now at the entrance of the Shelburne Museum in Shelburne, Vermont.

# BENNINGTON COUNTY

Called the Bridge of the Green, this bridge at West Arlington is of Town Lattice construction. Its span of 80 feet crosses the Battenkill River west off Route 7, next to Route 313. It was built in 1852, but the name of the builder is unknown.

*(Left)* The Chiselville Bridge is located about two miles east of Sunderland, just off Route 7. Built in 1870 by Daniel Oatman, it is of Town Lattice construction and has a span of 117 feet. Built too close to the river bed, the original bridge was washed out in the flood of 1869. It was rebuilt forty feet above the water, and a new center pier has since been added.

*(Right)* The Silk Bridge is found in Bennington, where it crosses the Walloomsac River northwest of town, next to Route 67A. It is of Town Lattice construction and has a span of 88 feet. Built in 1889 by Benjamin Sears, it is the oldest of three covered bridges left spanning the Walloomsac river.

Built in Bennington, the Henry Bridge is of Town Lattice construction. Northwest on Route 67A about a mile, it crosses the Walloomsac River with a span of 125 feet.

# CALEDONIA COUNTY

Near Lyndonville, we find the Randolph Bridge about three miles north of town, southeast off Route 114. It crosses the Passumpsic River and was built in 1865 by an unknown builder. Of Queenpost construction, it has a span of 66 feet and is still in use.

(*Left*) The Sanborn or Center Bridge, located west of North Lyndonville on Route 5, was built in 1869 of Paddleford construction by an unknown builder. Originally spanning 120 feet across the Passumpsic River, it was moved in 1960 to Lyndonville, where it is now a real estate office.

(*Right*) This bridge, the Portland Bridge, was located right in the middle of town crossing the Moose River in St. Johnsbury. Two other covered bridges made from the same plans were close by. One, the Works Bridge, was demolished in 1927. The other, the Goss Hollow Bridge, was built over the Sleeper's River in 1855 and was demolished in 1938.

(Left)  In the Lydonville area, John Clements, a noted stone mason, placed about thirty stone abutments where covered bridges were built. Many of them can still be seen although most of the bridges are gone. A remaining bridge, the Schoolhouse Bridge near Lyndon Center, was built in 1879 over the southern branch of the Passumpsic River by Lee Goodell. Spanning 42 feet, it can be found west off Route 5 on the South Wheelock Branch Road. Of the thirty or more covered bridges built in the Lyndonville area, only five are still in use.

(Right)  The Miller's Run Bridge, still in use, is also known as the Bradley Bridge. Built over the Miller's Run River on Route 122 near Lyndon Center, it is of Queenpost construction and spans 56 feet. It was built by E.H. Stone in 1878.

(*Left*)   Spanning the Black River near Hardwick, this old landmark has long since passed into time.

(*Right*)   A lovely small bridge, the Green Bank Hollow Bridge, is located just south of Danville, off Route 2, and 2½ miles into Caledonia County. It spans 50 feet across Joe's Brook and was built in 1866 of Queenpost construction by an unknown builder.

# CHITTENDEN COUNTY

The Lake Shore Bridge is located west of Charlotte, off Route 7, on the Lake Shore Road. This bridge was built by Leonard Sherman of Laminated Tied Arch construction.

(*Left*)  The Lower or Quinlan Bridge was built in 1849 by an unknown builder. Of Burr Arch construction, it spans 87 feet over Lewis Creek. It is located in East Charlotte, east off Route 7 on the road to North Ferrisburg.

(*Right*)  This old bridge stood in Hinesburg. Dr. Lewis J. Wainer remembers the bridge as a recreational site of the village youth who used to fish and swim beneath its sheltered deck. Long since gone, it is now replaced with a concrete-slab bridge.

The Upper Bridge in East Charlotte was built by an unknown builder in 1849. Of Burr Arch construction, it has a span of 58 feet over Lewis Creek, just east of Quinlan's Bridge.

# ESSEX COUNTY

The Mount Orne Bridge, located at Lunenburg, spans 285 feet over the Connecticut River. Rebuilt in 1911 by the Berlin Construction Company and Babbitt Brothers, the original bridge was washed away in 1905. It was partially wrecked twice during reconstruction by high waters.

*(Left)* Even the surrounding trees protecting this old bridge seem to be weeping at its passing. It was the old Crete Bridge in Canaan. Essex County remains the only county in Vermont with no covered bridges left standing.

*(Right)* Over the Connecticut River at Lemington, stands the Columbia Bridge. Built in 1912, the builder's name has been forgotten. The original bridge on this site was a toll bridge totally destroyed during a vicious storm. Rebuilt, the second ended in flames. The present bridge is reinforced with steel rods, beams, and concrete. One side is boarded for protection from the weather, and the other is open to let in light.

# FRANKLIN COUNTY

The Fuller Bridge spans 55 feet across Black Falls Creek north of Montgomery, next to Route 118. Built in 1890 by Sheldon and Savannah Jewett, it is of Town Lattice construction and was still in use until January 1983, when the boom of a log truck knocked out the roof rafters. The bridge, which had been extensively renovated in 1981, will be rebuilt.

(*Left*) The West Hill or Chrystal Springs Bridge is located just three miles south of Montgomery, off Route 118 where it crosses West Hill Brook on an abandoned road. Built by Sheldon and Savannah Jewett in 1883, it has a span of 40 feet. A natural waterfall flows at the bridge.

(*Right*) Many fishing bridges abound in the United States, with the most famous of all located in Yellowstone National Park. However, Vermont had its own fishing bridge located across a shallow creek entering St. Albans Bay in Lamoille County. A modern structure replaces this bridge, though tall tales of "whoppers" caught through holes in the deck may still be heard.

*(Left)* The Shingle Mill Bridge was located between East and West Enosburg. It was of Town Lattice construction.

*(Right)* The Comstock Bridge is found in Montgomery. This bridge is a prime example of the use of pointed abutments. Pointing means the process of forcing cement into the openings of the rocks and stones which compose the support of most abutments. This increases the strength of these abutments and helps to prevent deterioration. In this case, the abutments were both pointed, one side left the pointing showing and the other plastered over with a thick coating of cement. It was built in 1883 by the Jewett brothers who built most of the covered bridges still in use in the Montgomery area. There are more covered bridges still in use in this area than in any other in Vermont. The Comstock Bridge is of Town Lattice construction, and it spans 80 feet. A "must" for covered-bridge enthusiasts.

*(Left)* The Hectorville Bridge was built of Town Lattice construction in 1883 by Sheldon and Savannah Jewett. It has a span of 54 feet over the southern branch of the Trout River, about one mile west of Montgomery Center, off Route 118.

*(Right)* The Pierces Mills Bridge was located in Georgia Plains. Rather flimsily built originally, an A-shaped truss was later added to give it more strength. It has long since disappeared from the scene, and little more information has been forthcoming.

*(Left)*  The East Fairfield Bridge in East Fairfield is located over Black Creek South, next to Route 36. Of Queenpost construction, it was built in 1865 and has a span of 68 feet. The name of the builder has long been forgotten.

*(Right)*  Built in 1875 by Sheldon and Savannah Jewett, the Hopkins Bridge is of Town Lattice construction. It has a span of 80 feet over the Trout River, located west of Montgomery, next to Route 118.

# LAMOILLE COUNTY

The Fisher Railroad Bridge has been in use since its construction by the Pratt Construction Company in 1908. Located in Wolcott, it can be found south of town off Route 15. It has a span of 102 feet and is of Town Lattice construction. A cupola intended to vent engine smoke runs the entire length of the bridge and beams now support the deck. It has been thoroughly restored and is the only covered railroad bridge still in use in Vermont.

*(Left)* This lovely old bridge was located in Stowe. Unfortunately, even the name has been forgotten.

*(Right)* The Village or Church Street Bridge was built by an unknown builder in 1877. Of Queenpost construction and spanning 60 feet, it is located in Waterville where it crosses the Kelley River, west off Route 109.

(*Left*) Called Miller's Brook Bridge, this bridge used to be near Stowe. It was of Queenpost construction, but X-shaped braces were used for the middle supports so it should, actually, be called of Warren truss construction.

(*Right*) The popular Powerhouse or Schoolhouse Bridge stands just west of Johnson, next to Route 100C. Spanning 75 feet across the Gihon River, it was built of Queenpost construction in 1870 by an unknown builder. After heated demonstrations by the women of the town, it was renovated by William Locke in 1960.

Phil Ziegler '81

(*Left*) Long since a bridge of the past, this old Railroad Bridge stood near Cambridge Junction.

(*Right*) The completely restored Gold Brook Bridge is just east of Route 100, a mile or so south of Stowe, where it crosses Gold Brook. It was built by John N. Smith of Howe truss construction. Spanning 50 feet, railroad rails are used as cross beams under the deck — the only covered bridge in Vermont with this feature. Perpetual care is guaranteed.

(*Left*)  The Scott or Gristmill Bridge can be found east of Jeffersonville, off Route 108 on the Canyon Road. Its span of 80 feet crosses the Brewster Creek. Of Burr Arch construction, the building date and the builder have long been forgotten.

(*Right*)  The Scribner Bridge is in Johnson. It crosses the Gihon River just east of town next to Route 100C. Built in 1870, it has a span of 48 feet and is of Queenpost construction. It seems as if the covering was put on this bridge after the rest was constructed and repaired by William Locke in 1960.

(Left)  The Mill, Junction, or Lower Bridge in Belvidere Junction crosses the Kelley River just west off Route 109. Spanning 70 feet, it was built by Lewis Robinson in 1887 of Queenpost construction.

(Right)  The Waterman or German Bridge was built in 1868 by George Mills. Of Queenpost construction, it spans 87 feet over Waterman's Brook just south of Johnson, off Route 115 on the River Road.

(*Left*) The Jaynes, Upper, or Codding Hollow Bridge was built about 1887 by an unknown builder. Near Waterville, it spans 57 feet across the Kelley River, just east of Route 109.

(*Right*) The Morgan or Upper Bridge is found in Belvidere Corners, known locally as Belvidere Junction. Built in 1887 by Messrs. Robinson, Tracey, and Leonard, it is of Queen-post construction and spans 60 feet across the Kelley River, just west off Route 109.

*(Left)* This splendid old covered bridge spanned the Seymour River near Cambridge.

*(Right)* The old Cleveland Bridge stood near Moscow.

(Left)  Built in the shadows of Mount Mansfield in the Pleasant Valley area, the Safford Bridge stood in all its glory for many years. It was in Cambridge. Very sturdily built, it was of Queenpost construction with additional struts supporting the bottom cords high above the brook. Nevertheless, it eventually succumbed to the ravages of nature.

(Right)  The Poland Bridge is nestled into its surroundings like a pheasant snuggled in the tall grass. Located in Cambridge Junction, north off Route 15 on the bypass to Route 109, it crosses the Lamoille River with a span of 140 feet. It was built of Burr Arch construction by George W. Holmes in 1887.

*(Left)* This bridge was nearly dismantled and replaced with a steel and concrete bridge when the Webb family decided to include it in their Shelburne Museum. The drawing here depicts the bridge in its original location in northern Cambridge. The pieces were numbered and replaced at the entrance of the Museum exactly as the original bridge was constructed by Walter B. Hill. Considered to be the finest restored covered bridge in Vermont, it was originally built of Burr Arch construction by Farwell Weatherby spanning 168 feet over the Lamoille River.

*(Right)* The Gates Farm Bridge was built late in 1897 by George H. Holmes. It is of Burr Arch construction and has a span of 60 feet. In 1951 it was moved to its present location near East Cambridge, on the Gates Farm by the Vermont Highway Department, just east of Route 115.

# ORANGE COUNTY

The Hyde, or as it is sometimes called, the Kingsbury Bridge, is in South Randolph, where it crosses the Second Branch White River just west of town next to Route 14. Of Multiple Kingpost construction, it was built in 1904 with a span of 45 feet. The builder's name cannot be recalled. As of 1980 it has been completely restored.

(*Left*) Sayer's Bridge stands in Thetford, just south of Route 113A on Route 132. Date of construction is not known, but it was built by the great covered-bridge builder and designer, Herman Haupt, the inventor of the Haupt truss. Its span of 80 feet crosses the Ompompanoosuc River. In 1963 the bridge was repaired, as the "stringers" were replaced with steel beams and the floor slats reconstructed. A natural waterfall flows below the bridge.

(*Right*) The Union Village Bridge is located at Union Village, just north of the village on Route 132. Built in 1867 of Multiple Kingpost construction, this bridge still crosses the Ompompanoosuc River. The builder's name has been forgotten.

*(Left)* The Orford Bridge was in Fairlee. Built in 1856 over the Connecticut River, it was of Town Lattice construction. In 1898 the roof blew off and was replaced with shingles. In 1936, the bridge was dismantled and replaced with a modern steel-and-concrete bridge.

*(Right)* This old bridge called the Market Street Bridge stood in Tunbridge.

(*Left*)  No facts are available about the Cushman Bridge, which was located in Tunbridge. When the photograph from which this bridge was drawn was taken, it had already shown signs of "giving up the ghost."

(*Right*)  In Tunbridge, stands the Lower or Cilley Bridge. Of Multiple Kingpost construction, it was built in 1883. Its span of 55 feet crosses the First Branch White River, west of town off Route 110.

(*Left*)  The Gifford, or C. K. Smith, Bridge was built in East Randolph in 1904. It is of Multiple Kingpost Haupt truss construction. The builder is unknown. Its 50-foot span crosses the Second Branch White River located west of town next to Route 14. This drawing shows it in a state of disrepair which has since been taken care of.

(*Right*)  The Larking Bridge is in North Tunbridge. It is of Multiple Kingpost construction and was built by Arthur Adams in 1902. Its 55-foot span crosses the First Branch White River, just east of town off Route 110.

# ORLEANS COUNTY

This little jewel of a covered bridge stood in Westfield. Called the Taft Brook Bridge, it blended in with its surroundings so beautifully one would think God planted a seed and it grew into this bridge. Of Town Lattice construction, it stood for many years.

(*Left*)  The Black River Bridge is southwest of Coventry on Coventry Road.  Built over the Black River by John D. Colton in 1881, it is of Paddleford construction and spans 50 feet.

(*Right*)  The Lord's Creek Bridge can be found on the LaBond Farm near Irasburg.  A private bridge built in 1881 by John D. Colton over Lord's Creek, it is of Paddleford construction and still in use.

(*Left*) This bridge, which collapsed in 1958 and was later rebuilt, is called the River Road or Schoolhouse Bridge. It is located about one mile south of Big Falls over the Missisquoi River near North Troy. The introduction of buttressed sides made for an unusual rendition of the Town Lattice construction. It has a span of 99 feet.

(*Right*) Twin bridges were built where the Clyde River meanders through flat marshy meadows in East Charleston. For an unknown reason, each was built of different construction. These bridges have long since disappeared.

*(Left)* Nothing remains, not even memories, of this old bridge which was located in West Charleston.

*(Right)* Note the peaceful, glorious setting surrounding this beautiful old bridge which is gone forever. Located in Irasburg, nothing but a few memories remain.

Built near Irasburg in 1881 by Timothy Horton, this bridge was destroyed in 1938. Spanning the Black River, it was of Paddleford construction and known as the Upper Bridge.

# RUTLAND COUNTY

The Twin Bridges are found in Rutland. They cross East Creek and were built by Nicholas Powers in 1850 of Town Lattice construction. After the first bridge was built, an ensuing flood created another new channel, so a second bridge was built to span the new channel. When the Pittsford Dam broke in 1947, one was washed away, and the remaining bridge was condemned to traffic and is now used as a storage shed for road equipment, etc. for the town.

(*Left*)  The Billings Bridge stood in Rutland. Built over Otter Creek by Timothy Horton in 1831 of Town Lattice construction, it was destroyed in 1952.

(*Right*)  The Gorham Bridge is located in Pittsford on the Pittsford-Proctor Road. It spans 114 feet across the Otter Creek and was built by Nicholas Powers and Abraham Owen of Town Lattice construction. Major repairs were made in 1956.

(*Left*)  The Sanderson Bridge was built in 1838 by an unknown builder. It spans 132 feet across Otter Creek, off Route 7, on Pearl Street in Brandon.

(*Right*)  East of Florence stands the Depot Bridge, which is also known as the Florence Station Bridge. It is of Town Lattice construction and has a span of 121 feet across the Otter Creek, west off Route 7 on the Florence Road. In 1974, Samuel Carrera renovated the bridge and the abutments.

*(Left)* This is the old "76" Bridge that stood in Rutland. This drawing shows the old bridge's skeleton before it was covered during restoration. It was planned to replace this bridge with a modern steel and concrete one until the town fathers decided to have it renovated. Unfortunately, regardless of the effort, this bridge was demolished.

*(Right)* The Dean Bridge is found south of Brandon off Route 7. It is also known as the Upper Bridge. Built in 1840 by an unknown builder, it has a span of 136 feet over Otter Creek.

The Battleground Bridge in Warren was built in 1975 by the Battleground Condominium Development Company. It has a span of 65 feet over Mill Brook and is of Stringer construction. It is located next to the Mad River Glen ski area. Although not a true covered bridge, its superb design, size and construction, like the Quechee Bridge, have earned it a place in this book.

*(Left)* The Big Eddy Bridge, located just east of Waitsfield on Route 100, was built in 1853 of Burr Arch construction. It has a span of 113 feet over the Mad River and was restored in 1975 by Milton Gratton & Sons.

*(Right)* The Coburn or Cemetery Bridge is located northwest of East Montpelier, just off Route 2. Built in 1851 by Mr. Coburn, it crosses the Winooski River. Spanning 50 feet and of Queenpost construction, it was renovated by the Vermont Highway Department in 1974.

*(Left)* Not much is remembered about this lovely bridge located in Northfield Falls. It has a span of 55 feet over Lower Cox Brook and is called the Newell Bridge. Of Queen-post construction, it stands just west of Station Bridge, part of a group of covered bridges in the area.

*(Right)* The Moseley Bridge is located just west of Route 24 in Northfield. Crossing Stony Brook, it has a span of 39 feet. It was built of Kingpost construction in 1899 by John Moseley.

(*Left*)   This old bridge, the Wilder Bridge, was located in Waitsfield, where it crossed the Mad River. No other information is available.

(*Right*)   The Orton Farm Bridge is in Marshfield. It crosses the Winooski River east of town off Route 2. Built by Herman Townsend in 1890 of Queenpost construction, it has a span of 50 feet. For those who may remember, this bridge was originally called the Martin Bridge.

(*Left*) Nothing seems to remain but a few old photographs of this old Waitsfield bridge.

(*Right*) The old High Bridge, also known as the Palmer Bridge, was built in 1855. Located in Waitsfield, the builder's name has long been forgotten. This bridge of Queenpost Truss, Tied Arch construction, lasted for 103 years but was destroyed in 1958.

(Left) This old bridge was in Warren. It has been gone a long time and even the name has been forgotten.

(Right) The Upper Bridge in Northfield Falls is of Queenpost construction and has a span of 42 feet. It crosses Cox Brook just west of the Newell Bridge. Although the bridge is still used, the year it was built and the name of the builder have been forgotten.

(*Left*)  Another old bridge which has passed into history was this bridge near Middlesex, where it crossed the Black River.

(*Right*)  This was the Thatcher Brook Bridge near Waterbury.

Phil
Ziegler
82

(*Left*) Not even the name can be recalled by old timers in Riverton, where this bridge was located.

(*Right*) Kent's Corner Bridge is known as Kent's Museum. It was built in 1963 of Kingpost construction and has a span of 22 feet over Curtis Brook. To find it, go west off Route 14 at Kent's Corner in Calais.

The Station Bridge near Northfield Falls is of Town Lattice construction and has a span of 100 feet over the Dog River. The date of construction and the builder are unknown. One of three bridges within ¾ mile, it is just off Route 12 going west. The Newell Bridge can be seen just west of the Station Bridge. This is the only place in New England where two covered bridges can be seen at once.

Worral's Bridge is south of Bartonsville. It was built in 1868 by Sanford Granger. Its 87-foot span crosses the Williams River just east off Route 103. The bridge has a wooden ramp to the roadway on the west end, which is a very unusual feature.

*(Left)* The Twin Silos or High Mowing Farm Bridge is a more recently constructed bridge. Built in 1949 in Wilmington by the Hayes Brothers, it stands just east of town off Route 100 on High Mowing Farm. It is of Town Lattice construction and spans 22 feet.

*(Right)* The Kidder Hill Bridge was built in 1870; the name of the builder has been forgotten. It stands in the center of town in Grafton, off Route 121. Crossing the southern branch of the Saxton's River, it spans 37 feet and is of Queenpost construction.

Phil Ziegler '81

(*Left*) Way back in the ox-team days, before the horse and buggy, there were many open bridges — bridges that had no side boardings or roofs. This Open Bridge, which was located in West Dover, was a perfect example. You will note that although an open bridge, much care was taken to make it attractive. No examples of this type of bridge remain, although they were used long after the covered bridge came into use.

(*Right*) Lewis or Cobbs Brook Creek Bridge stood in Westminster. Crossing Lewis Creek, it was built by Sanford Granger in 1838. Originally, it was 41 feet long, but in 1843 an additional span of 24 feet was added, making a total span of 65 feet. It was destroyed in 1943.

*(Left)* The town of Guilford now stores its equipment in this attractive old bridge. Please note its neatly trimmed arch. It crosses the Green River, but was condemned as being unsafe for traffic.

*(Right)* The Williamsville Bridge was built in 1860 by Caleb Lamson. Of Town Lattice construction, it has a span of 120 feet over the Stony or Marlboro Brook. Now completely restored, it can be found west off Route 30 on the Williamsville–South Newfane Road.

(*Left*)  In 1949, this bridge, the Village Bridge in Saxton's River, was replaced with a modern bridge. Built in 1870 by an unknown builder, it crossed Saxton's River.

(*Right*)  Called Wardsboro Bridge, this lovely old bridge was found near Newfane.

(*Left*)  The covered railroad bridges were tall, narrow, and considered to be generally somewhat ugly. However, the covered railroad bridge at Bellows Falls broke this pattern of ugliness. The builder faced the portals with a lovely design of bricks and followed the form of the arched trusses with vertical planks. The bridge was abandoned many years ago.

(*Right*)  The now-restored Creamery Bridge can be found south of Brattleboro, near Route 109. Many builders participated in the construction of this bridge in 1878. Of Town Lattice Construction, it crosses Whetstone Brook. A sidewalk was added to the bridge in 1917. In the early 1900s, a new slate roof was added; its original cost was $1037.80. This is a long cry from what it would cost to build one like it today.

(*Left*) The Macmillan Bridge can be found by travelling a short distance out of Grafton on Townshend Road. The bridge crosses the Saxton's River (southern branch); it was built in 1967 with a span of 57 feet. However, this bridge is not, technically, a true covered bridge, but remains quite picturesque with its small dam and waterfall just upstream.

(*Right*) In West Dummerston stands the West Dummerston Bridge. Caleb B. Lamson built it in 1872. It is of Town Lattice construction and spans 280 feet. The longest covered bridge in Vermont, it crosses the West River just east of town next to Route 30.

(*Left*)  Its unusual portal design made the Village Bridge at Newfane stand out. Built in 1841, its mortarless rock abutments held it up for almost one and a half centuries. It was replaced by a modern bridge mainly because the extra sharp curves at its portals made it dangerous for modern traffic.

(*Right*)  The William's Bridge was built in Bartonsville in 1870 by Sanford Granger. It has a span of 151 feet over the William's River and is of Town Lattice construction. To find this bridge, go north off Route 103 about a half mile.

# WINDSOR COUNTY

The Lincoln Bridge is the only Pratt truss constructed bridge left in Vermont. It can be found in West Woodstock, next to Route 4. Built over the Ottauquechee River in 1865, it spans 136 feet.

(*Left*)  The Middle Bridge is located in Woodstock, on Union Street. Built in 1969 by M.S. Gratton, it spans 125 feet over the Ottauquechee River. Of Town Lattice construction, it was severely damaged by fire in 1974 and completely restored — making it Vermont's newest Town Lattice covered bridge.

(*Right*)  Downer's or Upper Falls Bridge can be found at the junction of Route 106 and Route 144, just west of Perkinsville. Built in 1840, the original builder is unknown. Completely rebuilt in 1975–76 by Milton Gratton, it spans 121 feet across the Black River.

(*Left*) Of Laminated Arch construction, the Mill Brook Bridge stood in West Windsor over Mill Creek.

(*Right*) Houghton Bridge, a grand old example of the covered bridge, stood over Mill Brook near Brownsville.

(*Left*) Although not a true covered bridge, I included the Quechee Bridge in this book because of its lovely lines and beautiful setting. Built in 1970 at the Quechee Lakes development, its 90-foot span crosses the Ottauquechee River just north off Route 4.

(*Right*) In Chester, the Mill Bridge protected its crossing for almost a century.

*(Left)* The Taftsville Bridge located in Taftsville was built in 1835. Its Multiple Kingpost construction with additional Queenpost arches makes this bridge unique. No similar trusses stand in Vermont. Iron rods have been added for strength. Built by Solomon Edmunds, this bridge spans 190 feet over the Ottauquechee River, north of town next to Route 4. With a waterfall above the bridge dam, it lies in a most picturesque setting.

*(Right)* The Titcomb Bridge, built in 1880 by Henry and James Tasker, is of Multiple Kingpost construction and spans 46 feet and 6 inches. It crosses an unnamed brook. Removed in 1959, it was restored in 1963 by Andrew A. Titcomb, its present owner. Formerly known as the Stoughton Bridge, it is located north-east of Perkinsville where it crosses the Black River.

*(Left)* This old bridge, called the Cheshire Bridge, was a toll bridge between Springfield, Vermont and Charlestown, New Hampshire. A modern bridge replaced it many years ago.

*(Right)* Nature has won the battle of time with this lovely old Martin's Bridge which stood in Royalton. It appears to be disintegrating into the earth from whence its materials came.

(*Left*)   The old Chair Factory Bridge stood in South Royalton.

(*Right*)   Called the Perkinsville Bridge, this beautiful old bridge stood in Weathersfield, but has long since disappeared. Note the lovely portal design and the side openings. Much care went into the making of this bridge.